These questions are answered by:

____

____

____

All your answers are not wrong
All your answers are not always right
All come from your bright or dark thoughts
All come truly, deeply from your heart and soul
And all come to define who you are at this very moment

DAY 1

When was the first time you tried your own recipe?

DAY 2

What is it like to have a family?

DAY 3

What do you think makes a good career?

DAY 4

If you died tomorrow, what would you most be remembered for?

DAY 5

What's your biggest regret?

DAY 6

Is there anything you could do now differently in the present that would make you happier and improve your quality of life in the future? What are those?

DAY 7

What was the probability that something had to go wrong to be successful?

DAY 8

Would you rather have an official job or one that pays better? Why?

DAY 9

Do you prefer reading? Why?

DAY 10

What is the one thing you are least sure that you've spent the most time thinking about?

DAY 11

Some people say that life starts at 30. Why is that so?

DAY 12

What is the worst thing someone has done to you?

DAY 13

How do you deal with grief, anger, or sadness?

DAY 14

*How do you deal with being in a position where your life is
messed up and it's your decision?*

DAY 15

How long does it take you to get ready for work?

DAY 16

Do you often feel that you don't know anything? Why?

DAY 17

What kinds of stories would you tell about things you might not have told your future self?

DAY 18

If you are going to escape from a combat situation, what will be your most important tool or weapon?

DAY 19

Why would you rather have snow than rain?

DAY 20

How do you manage your own money? What is the one rule you follow?

DAY 21

Would you rather not have that choice?

DAY 22

How do you plan on going forward?

DAY 23

Which is your favorite thing about that experience and why?

DAY 24

Write about your favorite movie soundtrack.

DAY 25

Does the fact that you are sad makes you any less of a person?

DAY 26

What to do if you're caught in an airplane and aren't allowed to get off?

DAY 27

What's the matter? You're not feeling it?

How do you think you have handled your life?

Would you rather be dressed up or have your hair styled?

What are you looking forward to the most?

DAY 31

Why would you rather not be able to use the internet?

DAY 32

What is the most important change you made as a child?

DAY 33

When was the last time you climbed a tree just for fun?

DAY 34

Describe something you feel most passionate about to a complete stranger

DAY 35

What is one thing that you regret and what would you do differently?

DAY 36

If you were to die tomorrow, what would you want your last words to be?

DAY 37

What was your first big heartbreak like? How did you deal with it?

DAY 38

Are you the kind of person who's easy to get along with? Why?

DAY 39

What's one job you would never want to do?

DAY 40

What do you consider your greatest flaw?

DAY 41

If you could choose one thing about yourself, what would it be?

DAY 42

How long have you been working towards your dream and how much time have you allocated to it?

DAY 43

How do you think people would react if you were a superhero?

DAY 44

What do you wish you could have done differently when things went wrong?

DAY 45

If you could take one piece of advice from your parents, what would it be?

DAY 46

What would you do if you knew the answer to the pollution of the earth?

DAY 47

If you were able to choose one thing from your parents' past that you're most thankful you got to live through, what would it be and why?

DAY 48

What's something you've been known for?

DAY 49

If you could give another answer, a comment or a suggestion,
what would it be?

DAY 50

How do you keep your head above water on a bad day?

DAY 51

What are a few qualities you dislike in other people, and why?

DAY 52

If you had to choose one thing which would most annoy you to see on TV, what would you pick?

DAY 53

Would you rather fight a shark-filled river with a knife or a bow and arrow?

DAY 54

What should you learn?

DAY 55

What would you like to accomplish by the end of the year?

DAY 56

What is the one thing that will give you that extra edge?

DAY 57

List of things you've listened to in the past week

DAY 58

What would you do if you could only go to a foreign country and live there for the rest of your life?

DAY 59

What's your favorite game?

DAY 60

What is the best thing you could give a man/woman that could change his/her entire life?

DAY 61

What is the best thing to be doing if you have any interest or hope for something?

DAY 62

What would you say to someone who doesn't love you?

DAY 63

How do you deal with the lack of a proper, organized, disciplined plan?

DAY 64

Imagine that the world was colorless. How would that make
you feel?

DAY 65

Would you rather fight a battle with yourself and never be
defeated?

DAY 66

What would your 10 year old self will say to you now?

DAY 67

What would you do if you got a present you didn't like?

DAY 68

Who was one of the best friends you ever had?

DAY 69

What is the most important lesson you learned in childhood?

DAY 70

What is the worst thing you have ever done in your life?

DAY 71

How do you help your child learn to respect others?

DAY 72

Who do you want to be the very best person you can be?

DAY 73

List of things that you are not going to be in the next 48 hours

DAY 74

What do you want from your friends?

DAY 75

If you could travel through time, where would you go and why?

DAY 76

If you had to choose one thing to keep a secret from your friends, what would it be?

DAY 77

How do you deal with worry?

DAY 78

What is the one thing you do not want to be known for?

What would you say is the biggest challenge facing a young woman today?

What activities cause you to feel like you are living life to the fullest?

How would you describe the feeling of being keenly caught in the eye of a dabbling beauty?

DAY 82

Name a color after your favorite person.

DAY 83

Where does your creativity come from?

DAY 84

What is one thing you have in common with your favorite comedian?

DAY 85

What's funny to you?

DAY 86

What were the reasons you were told to keep silent?

DAY 87

Have you ever felt love that was undeniable? Why?

DAY 88

Would you rather have your life back, to be free of all of the trials and tribulations you've had to endure, or would you rather have the world of fiction that you knew but didn't understand? Why?

DAY 89

What is the best thing you have ever eaten?

DAY 90

How do you deal with the fact that you're not only in a competition where you have to be the best?

DAY 91

How do you deal with people who don't want to leave and don't understand the idea of letting go?

DAY 92

If you could take the current situation for 10 years and only change one thing, what would it be?

DAY 93

What is the one thing that doesn't get you upset?

DAY 94

What other people in your life do you wish you'd known?

DAY 95

What would you put in a time capsule to be opened by the next generation?

DAY 96

What is most important to you to create those hard-to-create moments of fear and terror that will become your keys to a happy life?

DAY 97

When does it become uncomfortable for you to not believe what you're being told?

DAY 98

If you could pick an image of the future for yourself and tell people that this is what the future looks like, what would you pick?

DAY 99

Does your senses, thought, beliefs, feelings, and thoughts, change? How?

DAY 100

Do you consider your appearance to be beautiful?

DAY 101

Do you have anything you want to say to someone? What is it?

DAY 102

Do you ever feel angry that you can't do something? Why?

DAY 103

What's the least bad thing you've ever done?

DAY 104

How have you changed the most?

DAY 105

How strong you think you are?

DAY 106

If you could go back in time to the day you were born, how would it happen?

____

____

____

____

____

DAY 107

How would you change the world to make it better?

____

____

____

____

____

DAY 108

What actions in your life will have the longest reaching consequences? How long will those effects be felt?

____

____

____

____

DAY 109

List of things that are listed as things you don't do

DAY 110

List of things that you haven't done yet but were checked by someone else

DAY 111

Which decade of clothing fashion was your favorite and least favorite?

When have you been courageous for yourself? When have you been courageous for others?

What have you done that has surprised you?

If you had to choose one thing that you could do over again, what would it be?

DAY 115

What were the main challenges you've faced and how did you solve each of them?

DAY 116

What's the best thing that happened this year?

DAY 117

How do you deal with bad people?

DAY 118

How do you deal with an unhinged fan base?

DAY 119

How do you deal with the bad taste and bad ideas?

DAY 120

Would you rather be called a girl from now on and have some fun like the last three girls of your life or do you want to be a person of your own choosing and live life fully yours? Why?

DAY 121

How would you feel if a new child moved into your neighborhood?

DAY 122

Which disease known to humankind do you hate the most? Explain why.

DAY 123

What do you like most about your current workplace?

DAY 124

What do you most dislike most about your past?

DAY 125

How would you describe the feeling of being pure?

DAY 126

Say something about what you're trying to say here

DAY 127

How would you describe the feeling of being caught in your natural groove?

DAY 128

Why did you give up on something you really wanted?

DAY 129

Who in your family is the biggest character?

DAY 130

What is one thing you have in common with these people in your space now?

DAY 131

If you could be anything in the world you want to be, what would you be?

DAY 132

If you had to choose one thing to take with you to the end (with no other things to take) what would you choose?

DAY 133

Why are humans so confident in beliefs that can't be proven?

DAY 134

Do you think of yourself as a worker, a consumer, a producer, or a promoter? Why?

DAY 135

Tell me about the happiest day of your life.

DAY 136

Do you ever wish on a star? Why or why not?

DAY 137

Which philosophers of your ancestors did you most admire?

DAY 138

When was the first time you realized it was going to be a disaster?

DAY 139

If you could travel anywhere in the world, where would it be?

DAY 140

What are your happy endings about, and where does your story start and end?

DAY 141

If you could only have one card, what would it be?

DAY 142

If you had to choose two changes to your life that could make it more effective, which would you choose and why?

DAY 143

Do you think a sixth sense exists? Explain.

DAY 144

If you could get out of this room, where would you go?

DAY 145

How do you deal with so many of the same problems in so many different ways?

DAY 146

How would you describe the feeling of watching someone doing something with incredible passion?

DAY 147

Describe your favorite dessert.

DAY 148

What is the one thing that has been thought to motivate creative thinking?

DAY 149

What do your sons think is good?

DAY 150

Do you have a quick and easy excuse? Why?

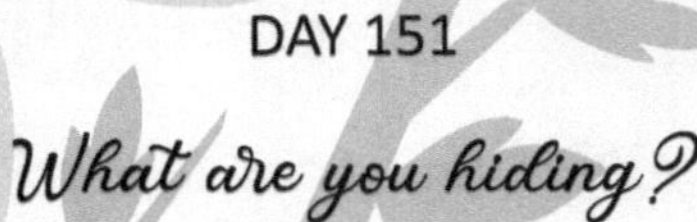

DAY 151

What are you hiding?

DAY 152

How can you teach your children to love other people?

DAY 153

Would you rather live in a glasshouse or a pigsty?

DAY 154

List of things that cause motion sickness

DAY 155

What's the most dangerous thing you've done?

DAY 156

What was your most embarrassing moment in the last four weeks?

DAY 157

If you could see the future of technology, which ones would you like to use?

DAY 158

What do you think about ghosts?

DAY 159

How are you feeling?

DAY 160

Who is one of the most interesting people you have ever met?

DAY 161

Tell about a time when you shocked someone.

DAY 162

What are your thoughts about tomorrow?

DAY 163

What is the one thing you believe in and will bet your whole life with it?

DAY 164

What do you want to be when you retire?

DAY 165

Would you rather forget who you are or not know who everyone else is? Why?

DAY 166

If you had to choose one thing in your list of things to learn, which one would you choose first?

DAY 167

Do you think it's strange?

DAY 168

Do you plan on giving away anything you're making and sharing with your friends? Why?

DAY 169

Would you rather live in a world with no division of tasks or a world with multiple choices for tasks? Why?

DAY 170

What is a convenience you wouldn't want to do without?

DAY 171

Why do you think you're going to tell how you're going to make a living?

DAY 172

If you could be what your parents had in mind, what would it be?

DAY 173

What's the one thing you've always wanted and never achieved?

DAY 174

What makes you comfortable in this city?

DAY 175

Do you have a particular fantasy of somebody else? Who is it?

DAY 176

What are your guilty pleasures?

DAY 177

How do you stop children from having bad feelings?

DAY 178

What happens when you laugh?

DAY 179

*Is "always the fastest" a productive or a nonproductive style?
Why?*

DAY 180

What's the meaning and story behind your username?

DAY 181

What are the top three things you wish?

DAY 182

If you had to choose one adventure, which would you choose?

DAY 183

Where do you look for inspiration?

DAY 184

How do you deal with people who are saying you shouldn't be here?

DAY 185

What might happen if you put the wrong kind of stress on a brain?

DAY 186

What is the one thing you're willing to sacrifice for and why?

DAY 187

What qualities would you want to have in a good child?

DAY 188

What's the hardest thing you've ever done in your life?

DAY 189

How would you describe the feeling of being all alone?

DAY 190

What other books would you recommend to others who are
searching for self-actualization?

DAY 191

What things do you think are beautiful?

DAY 192

Who are your favorite actors or artists of all time?

DAY 193

In detail, write about how you would like people to feel after interacting with you.

____
____
____
____
____
____

DAY 194

Which one of them are your real friends?

____
____
____
____

DAY 195

How do you deal with a situation that's coming up in your life?

____
____
____

DAY 196

Who are your favorite writers?

DAY 197

When did you find someone you really connected with?

DAY 198

If you had any warning. What would you have done differently?

DAY 199

What's the most ridiculous thing you've done?

DAY 200

Why was that role pivotal in your life?

DAY 201

What did you do on the beach?

What has been the most amazing part of your growing up experience?

If you had to move to another country, what things would you miss the most about where you live now?

How do you make money?

DAY 205

What's the difference between a physical touch and a verbal touch?

DAY 206

If you had to choose one thing that made the experience amazing for you the most, what would that be?

DAY 207

What's your favorite place to be in a group?

DAY 208

Discuss how a person achieves fame and fortune and how it changes the individual's life.

DAY 209

List of things that you want to stay away from

DAY 210

What is the most important thing you wish you had when you were younger that would have saved you?

DAY 211

Say something about your past and tell what that was it like.

DAY 212

Would you rather be a circus clown? Why?

DAY 213

What scares you the most?

DAY 214

What are you looking forward to about the next 365 days?

DAY 215

Are there times when you feel the world is unfair to you?
When was it?

DAY 216

What is the one thing you're most grateful for?

DAY 217

What if you're allowed to write a letter to "the one who got away"? What would you tell him/her?

DAY 218

What were your main lessons learned?

DAY 219

What was one of your happiest memories?

DAY 220

Are you taking the right approach? Why? Why not?

DAY 221

What did you teach your children about responsibility?

DAY 222

How do you get what you want in life?

DAY 223

What's the point of a rainbow?

DAY 224

When you were growing up, were you a fan of anything?
What are you a fan of?

DAY 225

List of things that will make you talk

DAY 226

What are the greatest vacations you have taken and what lessons can you take from it?

DAY 227

Describe a time when you could not afford something you deeply desired.

DAY 228

What are your two least favorite hobbies right now?

DAY 229

If you had to choose one thing to change in the next 5 years, what would be your pick?

DAY 230

What would you tell a friend who is telling you something that you knew that he or she is wrong?

DAY 231

Why do you use so many words?

DAY 232

What were the breaks in your life?

DAY 233

*If you could be one thing for just one day what would it be
and why?*

DAY 234

List of things that make you breath harder

DAY 235

What can you do to have your voice heard?

DAY 236

If you could take back one item from your childhood, what would it be?

DAY 237

What did you say today that made you laugh?

DAY 238

Look at yourself in the mirror and describe what you see.

DAY 239

Which is easier, to love or be loved? Why?

DAY 240

How comfortable are you in bed?

DAY 241

Do you treat the joy of getting things done as an end in itself,
or as a precondition for deeper, more meaningful experiences?

DAY 242

How did you do it?

DAY 243

List of things that would be easy to fix

DAY 244

When was the first instance you realized you have a problem and needed to look for solutions?

DAY 245

List of things that you built in your mind

DAY 246

Which character would you create to represent your favorite drink?

DAY 247

If you could spend a lifetime in a city, where would you live?

DAY 248

List of things that are really "last week's news"

DAY 249

What is the most horrible thing you can imagine happening to someone?

DAY 250

What is one thing you would most prefer to improve in your life?

DAY 251

What is worth doing in the face of hardship?

DAY 252

How do you deal with being depressed?

DAY 253

If you had to choose one thing that would make you the happiest, what would it be?

DAY 254

Would you rather have a cup of cold tea with your coffee or a cup of hot tea with your coffee?

DAY 255

Would you rather be among the best? Why?

DAY 256

What if it's your last day on earth? How would you spend it?

DAY 257

What was it like to do it?

DAY 258

Do you like commercials? Tell about your favorite commercial.

DAY 259

Are you the kind of person who believes in miracles, fairy dust, or wishes coming true? Why?

DAY 260

Do you feel tired? Why?

DAY 261

Tell me about some of the lessons the school of life has taught you so far.

DAY 262

What are your biggest goals this year?

DAY 263

How would you describe the feeling of experiencing your first fantasy?

DAY 264

How do you deal with that situation where you've spent your entire life fighting for what you believe in?

DAY 265

If you had to choose the most valuable lesson you've never learned, which would it be?

DAY 266

Would you like to buy anything for yourself? Why?

DAY 267

What do you do on a regular day?

DAY 268

What's your first reaction when you're told that someone is going to be your first-ever partner in the bedroom?

DAY 269

If you didn't go out on a date this weekend, what are you doing instead?

DAY 270

What was you happiest when you were little?

DAY 271

If you could choose between your health or your money, which would you choose and why?

DAY 272

Have you ever had the desire to meet your favorite movie stars? Why or why not?

DAY 273

Where are you now, by the way?

DAY 274

What is the one thing that makes your life a lot better than it used to be?

DAY 275

What is one thing about life and why should you make a difference?

DAY 276

How would you describe the feeling of being part of an amazing family?

DAY 277

How does your mind stay focused when everything else starts to fall apart?

DAY 278

Do you love being involved with other people? Why?

DAY 279

If you had to choose one thing today to be your life goal, what would it be?

DAY 280

What is the best thing you could possibly eat today?

DAY 281

What do you do when you're a plant?

DAY 282

What makes you think the other person is a monster and not a friend?

DAY 283

Would you rather have that man or a dog in your home?

DAY 284

Would you rather have no sense of smell or smell everything around you with extra ability? Why?

DAY 285

Are you happy with who you are in your current profession?

What is unfair to you?

List of things that matter

What would you like the most?

DAY 289

If you could have anything, what would it be?

DAY 290

If you had to choose one artist to have in your life, who would it be and why?

DAY 291

What makes you most ashamed?

DAY 292

Would you rather fight or give up your seat? Why?

DAY 293

List of things that you want to change.

DAY 294

What's your strangest experience?

DAY 295

Are you afraid of being alone? Why?

DAY 296

What advice would you give your future self?

DAY 297

What are you still struggling with as of late?

DAY 298

What is one thing not to do with a robot?

DAY 299

What do you think is the greatest invention in your lifetime and why?

DAY 300

How do you deal with people who don't see the same way you see them?

DAY 301

What's your favorite way to do anything?

DAY 302

What did you think was the most important event in your life?

DAY 303

What do you think the most important life lesson is?

DAY 304

What do you do during the day to make yourself happy?

DAY 305

What did you feel like you could have changed more?

DAY 306

Do you have a lot of real friends? How many?

DAY 307

Would you rather have it the way it is?

DAY 308

What has been your greatest accomplishment to date?

DAY 309

Would you rather have to do things your way or get the experience?

DAY 310

What is the one thing that you are not in love with?

DAY 311

What is one thing you love about your country?

DAY 312

What was it you were thinking about?

DAY 313

How do you make mistakes?

DAY 314

Would you rather be a little bit younger or a little bit older?

DAY 315

What is the one thing you wish your enemies would remember about you?

DAY 316

What is your idea of a boring evening?

DAY 317

What is one of your top priorities for your life?

DAY 318

How did you spend your free time? Why?

DAY 319

What is the one thing you most regret doing?

DAY 320

What is one thing you have in common with your worst sports hero?

DAY 321

If you could pick one or two things that you would change about your habits, what would they be?

DAY 322

If you could turn everything upside down, what would come up?

DAY 323

Recall a time when you found yourself in a perilous situation. Tell the story of how you got into that situation and how you survived it.

DAY 324

List of things that you are going to do here

DAY 325

How would you describe the feeling of being informed?

DAY 326

If you could return in time to a set time to relive it, but not change anything, what would you choose and why?

DAY 327

What is your vision for your life?

DAY 328

List of things you hate to wear

DAY 329

How are you like one of your brothers or sisters?

DAY 330

What is the one thing you have learned about yourself over the years that you feel most proud of?

DAY 331

What are you really trying to accomplish?

DAY 332

What is most important to you, to be or not to be?

DAY 333

*If you had to choose one thing you're most grateful for in all
the world, what would it be?*

DAY 334

What is the most significant book you've read recently and why?

DAY 335

Do you want to make a difference in the world? Why?

DAY 336

What sort of person do you want to become?

DAY 337

What is something that made your mother happy?

DAY 338

What if you lost your ability to speak? What would you do?

DAY 339

List of things that you want to talk about

DAY 340

What is the one thing that makes you different from all your friends?

DAY 341

What's your first reaction when you see a new species?

DAY 342

Why do you have a unique personality trait?

Do you enjoy hearing stories about someone other than yourself?

Where's your favorite spot to get a good night's sleep?

If you could have only three things in your office or on your desk, what would it be and why?

DAY 346

If you were a superhero, what would you do bad?

DAY 347

What do you use to cope when you're feeling uncomfortable?

DAY 348

What is the biggest one you worry about for the next three years?

DAY 349

Have you done anything to get in trouble since you were a kid?

DAY 350

Are you a good listener? Why?

DAY 351

What are your biggest successes?

DAY 352

Describe yourself in one word or phrase

DAY 353

Tell a story about the things that you think are important.

DAY 354

What is the one thing you can do for humanity?

DAY 355

Would you rather stay as you are and die a thousand times or live as you want to live and make one more attempt at life?

DAY 356

Do you prefer to go to the store and pick up things or would you rather just buy goods?

DAY 357

What is the most significant technological change that will fundamentally change our lives?

What is a great night like?

What 'excess baggage' are you carrying around?

What exactly is 'The Truth'?

DAY 361

If you had to choose one thing from your childhood that you would want back, what would it be?

DAY 362

Would you rather work with a robot or a person?

DAY 363

Why are you up late more than most people having dark thoughts?

DAY 364

List of things that may or may not exist

DAY 365

If you could be in the right place at the wrong time, which would you choose?

DAY 366

What if someone asks you to break up with your significant other? What would you do?